Where did they come from?   Moab.   How long will their trip take?   Six days of walking, walking, walking.

This book is dedicated to my mother, Ruth, and my sister, Kathy, who took care of her.

Dear Children,

The story of Ruth and Naomi is from the Book of Ruth in the Bible.

The story is longer, and more complicated, than the one I have simplified here for children ages 4 to 8. When you get older, I hope you will read the longer version. It's good.

Barley is a grain, like rice and wheat. You might eat it in soup or as a vegetable side dish. Barley flour is used to make barley bread. Interestingly, Bethlehem means "House of Bread." Please read the directions for singing the harvest songs. The music starts as Ruth and Naomi near Bethlehem.

Because this story takes place in the country, I have chosen rabbits to comment at the bottom of the page. Please read their words last, just before you turn the page.

Best wishes,
Jean Marzollo

Grateful thanks to Sheila Rauch for designing the rabbits; Shelley Thornton; Rev. T. Richard Snyder; Rabbi Stacy Schlein; Helen Frenkley of Neot Kedumim— The Biblical Landscape Reserve in Israel; Irene K. Seff; Betsy Polivy; Patricia Adams; Irene O'Garden; Judith Kurz Foster; Bunny Hoffinger; Grace Kennedy; Molly Friedrich; Simone Kaplan; Barry O'Connell; Sr. Cathy Molloy; Ziggy Rees; Chalupa; my sons Dan and Dave; and my husband Claudio. I'd also like to thank the folks who help me so much at Little, Brown and Warner Faith, and lastly the children at the First Presbyterian Church of Philipstown; the Abraham Joshua Heschel School; St. Joseph's Catholic School; the Westchester Jewish Center Nursery School; the Ringwood Christian School; and Nice Care Day Care.

Little, Brown and Company • Time Warner Book Group
1271 Avenue of the Americas, New York, NY 10020
Visit our Web site at www.lb-kids.com

First Edition

ISBN 0-316-74139-6

10 9 8 7 6 5 4 3 2 1

SC

Manufactured in China

The illustrations for this book were painted in watercolor and Chinese ink, then scanned and finished in Adobe Photoshop on a Power Mac G4. The text was set in Hadriano Light and Kid Print, and the display type was set in Sand.

Do the arrows on the map show where Ruth and Naomi walked? Yes. They never hopped? No

A BIBLE STORY
:rated by JEAN MARZOLLO

Ruth and Naomi

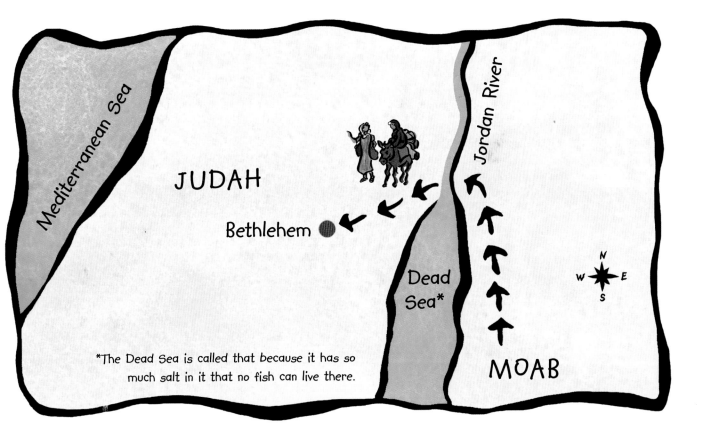

Mediterranean Sea

Jordan River

JUDAH

Bethlehem

Dead
Sea*

MOAB

N
W · E
S

*The Dead Sea is called that because it has so
much salt in it that no fish can live there.

LITTLE, BROWN AND COMPANY
New York · Boston

How did they get across the Jordan River?   They waded.   Where they crossed, it wasn't deep.

The reason why Ruth and Naomi began walking, walking, walking all the way to Bethlehem is that they were moving there to live. Ruth and Naomi were widows. A widow is a woman whose husband has died. Naomi's sons had died, too. Ruth had been married to one of Naomi's sons.

With no husband, no children, and no grandchildren, Naomi felt lonely. She decided to move back to Bethlehem, where she was born. She once had a house there. Maybe, just maybe, she could live there again.

Ruth knew that moving to Bethlehem would be very difficult for her mother-in-law. So, Ruth made a big decision. She would move to Bethlehem, too, in order to help Naomi.

Wherever you go, I will go.
Wherever you live, I will live.
Your people shall be my people,
And your God my God.

Ruth left the place where she was born to move to the place where Naomi was born.

She is loving and brave!

Every night on their trip, Ruth boiled barley grains to make soup, which was all the food they had. Being widows, Ruth and Naomi were very poor. Tomorrow, at last, they would reach Bethlehem. Then what? As the women fell asleep, they kept their thoughts to themselves because they didn't want to worry each other.

My house will be a wreck.

Was I right to leave my family in Moab?

Will Ruth like Bethlehem? Will she miss her home in Moab?

Will I ever be able to make Naomi happy?

It will be so embarrassing to tell my old friends in Bethlehem that I've come back with no husband, no children, and no grandchildren.

Will I ever be happy again?

Will people in Bethlehem be mean to me because I'm from Moab?

I'm so angry at God!

And I'm so hungry!

Where will I get food for us to eat? We have no money!

Why would people in Bethlehem be mean to people from Moab?   Long ago, they fought wars.   Some people never forget.

The next day, as Ruth and Naomi neared Bethlehem, they saw people harvesting barley. Men were cutting the barley with sharp, round knives called sickles. Women were tying it into sheaves for easy carrying. As they worked, they were singing.

Sing to the tune of "The Farmer in the Dell." Choose either the simple harvest word or the harder one in parentheses.

We cut (reap) the barley so,
We cut (reap) the barley so,
Praise God for barley-o,
We cut (reap) the barley so.

We tie (sheave) the barley s
We tie (sheave) the barley s
Praise God for barley-o,
We tie (sheave) the barley

Naomi, what are the two people near the road doing?

They are gleaning. The law here says that whatever the sheavers miss or drop must be left for the poor to find, or glean.

...at law helps poor people have food to eat.   I don't think rabbits have such nice laws.   We don't have laws, period!

As Ruth and Naomi approached the center of Bethlehem, they found people staring at them. Suddenly, a voice called out.

Naomi, is that YOU?

Yes, but don't call me Naomi anymore. Call me Mara, which means "bitter." My husband and sons died. I have no grandchildren. This is my daughter-in-law Ruth. She is a Moabite. We have no food left. Is my house still here?

Naomi's house was just barely standing. The roof had fallen in, and the walls had crumbled, but Ruth knew they could make it whole again. She felt good that their journey was over, but Naomi seemed sadder than ever. Ruth tried to cheer her up.

I'm not going to call you Mara, Naomi. Naomi means "happy," and someday you will be happy.

I doubt it, but I will say this. Ruth means "friend," and you surely are a friend to me, Ruth.

Next morning, without waking Naomi, Ruth left for the barley fields to glean fallen barley. She felt shy, so she stayed by herself, hoping no one would notice her. Most of the farm workers paid no attention, but some of the men teased her. Ruth tried to ignore them and focus on finding barley. There wasn't much left.

Presently, Farmer Boaz, the owner of many fields, came by. He looked over his land, and he was very pleased.

Farmer Boaz rode over to Ruth. He could see how frightened she was.

I am Farmer Boaz, Ruth, and this is my land. I will ask my farm workers to help you. When you are thirsty, please drink from my jars. I know that you left your home to help Naomi. May God reward you!

Thank you, Farmer Boaz. You are kind to speak so nicely to me, a stranger from Moab.

Farmer Boaz invited Ruth to sit with him and the other workers at lunch. He gave her barley bread and roasted barley grains to eat—enough for her to have some left over to save for Naomi. When Farmer Boaz thought Ruth wasn't listening, he spoke to his workers.

Women, please invite Ruth to follow right behind you. Drop some extra stalks for her. Men, stop being rude!

Sorry, Farmer Boaz!

We didn't mean any harm.

At the end of the day, a very tired but happy Ruth brought Naomi a full basket of gleaned grain, roasted grain, and barley bread.

I gleaned at fields owned by the nicest man: Farmer Boaz. He invited me to glean there throughout the harvest!

Praise God! Farmer Boaz is a cousin of my late husband.

That basket of barley treats is cheering Mara up.   Maybe one day she'll let people call her Naomi again.

Weeks passed. The barley harvest was nearly over. Every night Ruth brought food to Naomi.

Thank you, Ruth, for helping me so much. Now it's time for me to help you. I've been thinking . . . You should marry again.

But who could I ever marry that would be as wonderful as your son was?

Think, Ruth. Close your eyes. Is there not a man here in Bethlehem who has been extremely good to you?

Farmer Boaz has been very good to me, but he is a rich, important man here. He would never marry a Moabite!

Naomi convinced Ruth that Farmer Boaz would indeed marry her if Ruth would do exactly as Naomi told her. She told Ruth to bathe, put on the one good dress she had brought from Moab, and let Naomi fix her hair.

Tonight Farmer Boaz will be at the threshing floor. This evening is like a big work party. I want you to look your best, but don't let Farmer Boaz see you until he is done working and eating. When he rests, go over and visit him.

Are you serious?

Naomi is serious, all right.   That's a woman with a plan.   Does the plan work?   You'll find out . . .

Ruth heard singers as she climbed the hill to the threshing floor. Earlier in the day, barley had been spread out, and donkeys had dragged sleds across it to break it into grains and straw. The sleds had blades underneath, and children rode the sleds to weigh them down.

We break (thresh) the barley so,
We break (thresh) the barley so,
Praise God for barley-o,
We break (thresh) the barley so.

Now it was night. Singing with gusto, Farmer Boaz was tossing broken barley into the air. Wind blew the light straw away, but the precious barley grains were too heavy to be blown away. They fell to the ground, where Ruth helped others rake them into piles. Later, they would be stored in jars for food and seed.

We toss (winnow) the barley so,
We toss (winnow) the barley so,
Praise God for barley-o,
We toss (winnow) the barley so.

Farmers are so smart!   They use the wind to separate the grain from the straw!

Finally, the work party was over. The women went home, but the men stayed near the grain to protect it from robbers and animals. Ruth wanted to go home, too, but she had promised Naomi to visit Farmer Boaz, who was now sound asleep. Quietly, Ruth tiptoed over and knelt down near him. Farmer Boaz immediately awakened.

Ruth didn't know how to answer. Naomi had told her what to do but not what to say. Ruth thought quickly and decided to tell Farmer Boaz her true feelings.

Remember when you first met me? You said that you hoped God would reward me. Well, God did reward me by sending you to care for me.

Dear Ruth, I do care for you, and I believe God sent you to me! You are a wonderful woman, Ruth. Will you marry me?

What did Ruth say?   What do you think?

The wedding was a grand affair. God smiled on Ruth as she married Farmer Boaz. God smiled on Farmer Boaz as he took Ruth, the poor widow from Moab, for his wife. And God smiled on Naomi for having a good plan.

New barley sprouts were growing in the fields when Ruth and Farmer Boaz had their first baby, a son. At long last, Naomi had a grandchild. Her friends suggested the name Obed, which means "servant of God."

We name the baby so, We name the baby so,
Praise God for Obed-o! We name the baby so!

When Obed grew up,
he was the father of Jesse,
which means "wealthy."

When Jesse grew up,
he was the father of David,
which means "beloved one."

This David was the same
red-haired shepherd boy who
killed the giant, Goliath,
and later became
King of Israel.

This story goes from death to birth. The end is a new beginning. That's the circle of life! Rabbits have that, too!

Who's that?   David and his great-grandmother Ruth.   Listen . . . can you hear her?